Withdrawn

Rivers and Lakes

Yangtze River

Cari Meister

ABDO Publishing Company

visit us at
www.abdopub.com

Published by ABDO Publishing Company, 4940 Viking Drive, Edina, Minnesota 55435.
Copyright © 2002 by Abdo Consulting Group, Inc. International copyrights reserved in
all countries. No part of this book may be reproduced in any form without written
permission from the publisher.

Printed in the United States.

Photo credits: Corbis

Contributing editors: Bob Italia, Tamara L. Britton, Kate A. Furlong, Kristin Van Cleaf
Book design and graphics: Neil Klinepier

Library of Congress Cataloging-in-Publication Data

Meister, Cari.
    Yangtze River / Cari Meister.
      p. cm. -- (Rivers and lakes)
    Includes index.
    Summary: Surveys the origin, geological borders, water, plant and
animal life, and economic and ecological aspects of the Yangtze River.
    ISBN 1-57765-103-0
    1. Yangtze River (China)--Juvenile literature. [1. Yangtze River (China)]
I. Title. II. Series.
DS793.Y3M45 1999
951'.2--DC21   98-20923
                                                      CIP
                                                       AC

Contents

The Yangtze River

The Yangtze River is in China. It is Asia's longest river. It is 3,915 miles (6,300 km) long. This makes it the world's third-longest river. Only the Nile and Amazon Rivers are longer. The Chinese call the Yangtze *Chang Jiang*. *Chang Jiang* means Long River.

Many people live near the Yangtze. Some live in big, busy cities near the river's banks. Some live in rural villages and farm the land. Others live right on the water in floating cities.

The Yangtze River contributes much to China. Its waters are used to **irrigate** farmland. Dams on the river generate electricity. Boats transport people and goods along the Yangtze. This powerful river begins as a trickle in China's northeast mountains.

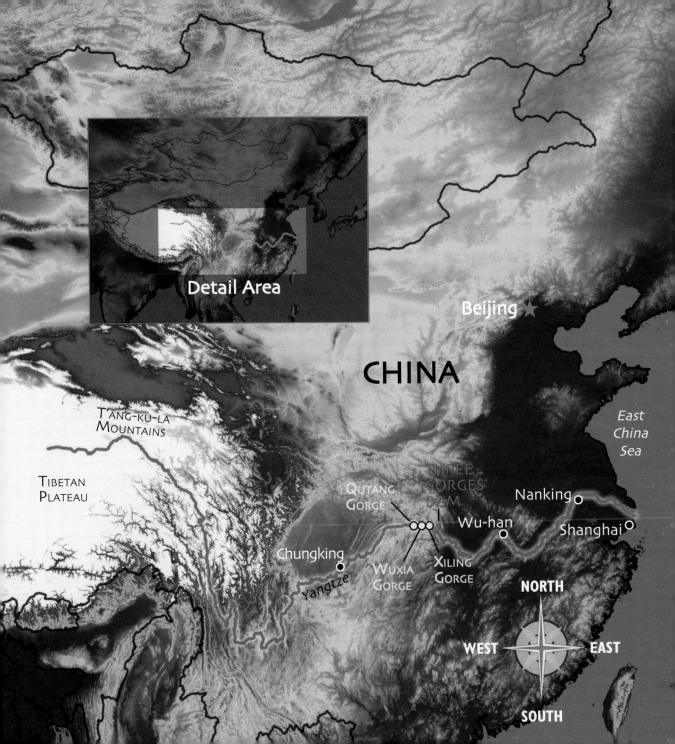

Detail Area

Beijing

CHINA

T'ANG-KU-LA
MOUNTAINS

TIBETAN
PLATEAU

East
China
Sea

Qutang
Gorge

THREE
GORGES
DAM

Nanking

Wu-han

Shanghai

Chungking

Wuxia
Gorge

Xiling
Gorge

Yangtze

NORTH

WEST

EAST

SOUTH

Humble Beginnings

*T*he Yangtze's **source** is high in the T'ang-ku-la Mountains on the Tibetan **Plateau**. In the T'ang-ku-la Mountains is a glacier called Jianggen Dirunan. As this glacier slowly melts, tiny droplets of water unite to form the mighty Yangtze River.

The Yangtze begins in the Xizang province and travels thousands of miles. It begins its journey in the mountains and flows through a wide valley. It connects with many lakes and **reservoirs**.

Farther along, the river reaches the eastern end of the highlands and flows through deep, narrow gorges. From there, the river enters the Three Gorges.

Opposite page: The Yangtze River
flowing through the Himalayas

The Three Gorges

*T*he Three Gorges are a series of large canyons in China. They have steep, sheer slopes that reach 2,000 feet (610 m) above the river's surface.

The first gorge is called Qutang. It is the shortest of the three gorges. It is about five miles (8 km) long. Here, the river flows quickly and contains many rapids and **eddies**.

The second gorge is called Wuxia. It is about 30 miles (48 km) long. Twelve peaks line this gorge. Each peak is associated with a Chinese legend.

The third gorge is called Xiling. Here, the steep cliffs often rise straight up from the water. In this gorge, the river contains many rapids and **shoals**.

After leaving the Three Gorges area, the Yangtze flows across low-lying plains. The river eventually empties into the East China Sea.

Two ships travel through the Qutang Gorge.

Animal Life

*T*he Yangtze River is home to many animals. Two of these animal species are very rare. They are the Chinese dolphin and the Chinese alligator.

The Chinese alligator, or *tu long*, lives in the lower river valleys. It is the smallest alligator species. Adults are only 7 feet (2 m) long, and weigh just 100 pounds (45 kg). There are only about 1,000 *tu longs* left.

The Chinese dolphin, or *baiji*, is a long-nosed dolphin. Pollution and dams on the river have reduced the number of *baiji*. Today, there are less than 100 *baiji* left.

Many fish also swim in the Yangtze. The Chinese sturgeon is one of the largest fish in the river. Sturgeon can grow to be 20 feet (6 m) long. Carp, catfish, and Chinese paddlefish also call the Yangtze home.

Chinese alligators have become rare in the Yangtze River. So scientists have learned to breed these alligators, such as the one below, in captivity. Scientists hope this will prevent the Chinese alligator from becoming extinct.

Plant Life

*T*he Yangtze and the surrounding land provide homes and food for many distinctive plants. Different types of algae plants grow in the river. Many fish eat this algae for their food.

In the river gorges, the golden larch grows on the hillsides. This tree has small, coin-shaped green leaves that turn yellow in the fall.

The kiwi plant is native to the Yangtze River valley in eastern China. In the early 1900s, **missionaries** took kiwi seeds to New Zealand. Today, kiwi fruits grow in many countries.

Lotus plants also grow in the eastern Yangtze valley, on the river's mud flats. The Chinese people enjoy the beautiful lotus flowers. The Chinese eat the lotus plant's roots as a vegetable. They also use the roots to make tea.

Lotus plants

People of the Yangtze

Many people live along the Yangtze. **Ethnic** Tibetans live in the western highlands. They are farmers. They raise animals and grow crops such as barley and rye.

The middle **plateau** is home to people who are a mixture of Chinese and other minorities. They make their living by farming, herding animals, and hunting.

The Yangtze's **delta**, at the East China Sea, has the country's greatest population. Most of the people who live on the delta are Chinese. They farm or work in the cities. Shanghai is on the Yangtze delta. It is China's largest city. More than seven million people live there.

Tibetans meet in the highlands near the Yangtze River.

An Economic Force

*T*he Chinese people depend on the Yangtze for many things. The river provides water for **irrigating** farmland. **Silt** left by receding floodwaters fertilizes the river **basin**. This fertile land produces half of China's crops. Almost all of China's rice grows there. Cotton, barley, corn, and beans are other common crops.

Many of China's most populous cities lie along the Yangtze. Shanghai, Wu-han, Chungking, and Nanking are among the largest. These cities are some of China's most important industrial centers.

The ports in these cities have created a large transportation network. The network moves goods and people from the coast to China's interior. This makes the Yangtze River China's principal waterway.

To power the cities and ports along the river, the Chinese have built dams. These dams generate **hydroelectric** power. But current dams cannot supply all the electricity the nation needs. So China's government has decided to build a dam at the bottom of the Three Gorges.

Tons of freight travel on the Yangtze River each year.

Three Gorges Dam

Construction of the Three Gorges Dam began in 1994. When it is completed in 2009, it will be Asia's biggest dam. The dam will be more than 1 mile (2 km) long and 600 feet (183 m) high. It will create a **reservoir** 365 miles (587 km) long.

Many people believe the dam will be beneficial. It will generate as much electricity as 15 nuclear power plants. The dam will prevent flooding downstream, which has been a problem throughout China's history. It will also allow big ships to travel farther up the river. This will help China's **economy** grow.

Other people think the dam is a bad idea. The reservoir the dam will create will destroy the homes of almost two million people. Also, valuable farmland and ancient **cultural** relics will be underwater. And changing the river's natural cycles will cause some plants and animals to become extinct, including the *baiji*. But the Chinese government has determined that the benefits of the dam are worth the costs.

A construction site at the Three Gorges Dam

The Yangtze's Future

*P*eople have lived in the Yangtze River valley for thousands of years. This area has always been important to China's people and **economy**.

Since 1950, China has worked to develop the economy of the Yangtze River **basin**. Industries have caused pollution in the river's water and the air around it. Clearing land beside the river for farming has caused soil **erosion**. This has caused too much **silt** to enter the water, which harms the plants and animals that live in and near the river.

China's growing economy and the possible effects of the Three Gorges Dam make the Yangtze's future uncertain. The health of the Yangtze must be considered in order for it to continue to support the people, plants, and animals that depend on it for survival.

Industrial factories, such as this coal plant,
have polluted the Yangtze's water and air.

Glossary

basin - low-lying land.

culture - the customs, arts, and tools of a nation or people at a certain time.

delta - an area of land at the mouth of a river formed by the deposit of silt, sand, and pebbles.

economy - the way a nation uses its money, goods, and natural resources.

eddy - a current within a larger current in a body of water, usually with a circular movement.

erosion - gradual wearing, rubbing, or washing away of the earth's rock or surface.

ethnic - a way to describe a group of people who have the same race, nationality, or culture.

hydroelectric - electricity that is generated when water flows through huge engines called turbines.

irrigate - to supply land with water using canals, channels, or pipes.

missionary - a person sent by his or her church to spread his or her religion to other people.

plateau - a raised area of flat land.

reservoir - a natural or man-made place that stores water.

shoal - a sandbar or sandbank that can be seen at low tide.

silt - fine sand or clay carried by water that settles on the land after a flood.

source - a spring, lake, or other body of water where a river or stream begins.

How Do You Say That?

Jianggen Dirunan - JEEYEN-gun dee-JUHR-uhn-ahn
plateau - plah-TOH
Qutang - CHOO-tang
reservoir - REZ-ehv-wahr
Shanghai - shang-HI

Wuxia - WOO-shya
Xiling - SHEE-leeng
Xizang - SHEED-zahn
Yangtze - yang-SEE

Web Sites

The Three Gorges Dam
http://www.timeforkids.com/tfk/magazines/story/0,6277,89377,00.html
Learn more about the Three Gorges Dam at this site from *Time Magazine for Kids*.

Chinese Dolphin
http://crucial.ied.edu.hk/dolphin/default.html
A great site from the Hong Kong Institute of Education. Learn about the endangered Chinese dolphin. Explore history, anatomy diagrams, habits, and more!

These sites are subject to change. Go to your favorite search engine and type in Yangtze River for more sites.

Index